My Cat

British Shorthair

Sara Cucini

AV2
www.openlightbox.com

AV2

Step 1
Go to **www.openlightbox.com**

Step 2
Enter this unique code

ARZGUQNXM

Step 3
Explore your interactive eBook!

AV2 is optimized for use on any device

Your interactive eBook comes with...

- **Audio** — Listen to the entire book read aloud
- **Videos** — Watch informative video clips
- **Weblinks** — Gain additional information for research
- **Try This!** — Complete activities and hands-on experiments
- **Key Words** — Study vocabulary, and complete a matching word activity
- **Quizzes** — Test your knowledge
- **Slideshows** — View images and captions
- **Share** — Share titles within your Learning Management System (LMS) or Library Circulation System
- **Citation** — Create bibliographical references following APA, CMOS, and MLA styles

This title is part of our AV2 digital subscription

1-Year K–2 Subscription
ISBN 978-1-7911-3310-8

Access hundreds of AV2 titles with our digital subscription.
Sign up for a FREE trial at **www.openlightbox.com/trial**

The digital components of this book are guaranteed to stay active for at least five years from the date of publication.

My Cat

British Shorthair

CONTENTS

2 AV2 Book Code
4 Like a Teddy Bear
6 A Large Cat
8 Round Eyes and Thick Fur
10 British Shorthair Kittens
12 Petting My Cat
14 Children and Dogs
16 Long Claws
18 The Doctor
20 Food and Attention
22 Fantastic British Shorthairs
24 Key Words

My British shorthair is very independent. Her round face and short fur make her look like a teddy bear. I love playing with her.

British shorthairs are large cats. They can weigh up to 16 pounds (7 kilograms). This is about as heavy as a bowling ball.

My cat has round, orange eyes. Her fur is gray and very dense.

CAT FUR LENGTH

No Fur

Sphynx

Short Fur

British Shorthair

Long Fur

Norwegian Forest Cat

My cat was very small when she was a kitten.

Her eyes were blue when she was born. They changed color over time.

My British shorthair does not like to be held. I pet her while she sits close to me.

Where in the World?

British shorthairs first arrived in Great Britain about 2,000 years ago.

British shorthairs are very curious.

My cat likes to follow me around the house.

She gets along well with children, and even with dogs.

My cat’s claws are long and sharp. My parents help me trim them every two weeks.

VERY IMPORTANT TOOL

Use a **brush** once a week to keep your cat's coat clean.

Once a year, I take my cat to see her doctor.

The doctor gives her medicine and makes sure that she is healthy.

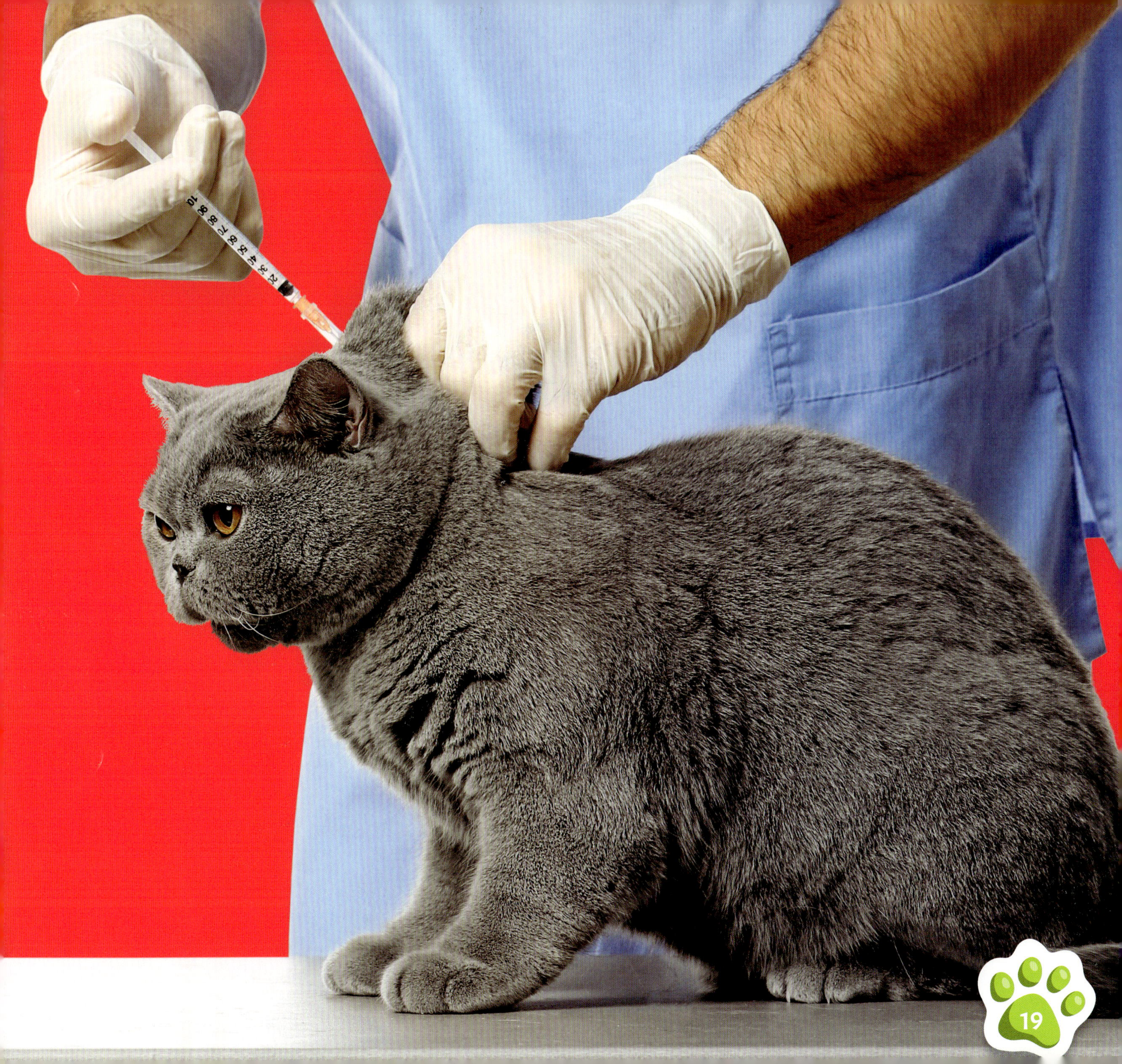

My cat should not eat too much. I feed her twice a day.

My cat is happy and relaxed. I give her healthy food and plenty of attention.

FANTASTIC BRITISH SHORTHAIRS

British shorthairs with **dark gray** coats are said to be "**blue**" in color.

The **Cheshire Cat**, a character in ***Alice's Adventures in Wonderland***, may have been inspired by a British shorthair.

British shorthairs can live to be **20 years old**.

A British shorthair won the **"Best in Show"** prize at one of the first cat shows ever held, in **1871**.

KEY WORDS

Research has shown that as much as 65 percent of all written material published in English is made up of 300 words. These 300 words cannot be taught using pictures or learned by sounding them out. They must be recognized by sight. This book contains 71 common sight words to help young readers improve their reading fluency and comprehension. This book also teaches young readers several important content words, such as proper nouns. These words are paired with pictures to aid in learning and improve understanding.

Page	Sight Words First Appearance
5	a, and, face, her, I, is, like, look, make, my, very, with
6	about, are, as, can, large, they, this, to, up
9	eyes, has, long, no
10	she, small, was, when
11	over, time, were
13	be, close, does, first, in, me, not, the, where, while, world, years
14	around, follow, house
15	along, children, even, gets, well
16	every, help, them, two
17	important, keep, once, use, your
18	gives, see, take, that
20	day, eat, much, should, too
21	food

Page	Content Words First Appearance
5	British shorthair, fur, teddy bear
6	bowling ball, cats
9	Norwegian forest cat, sphinx
10	kitten
11	color
13	Great Britain
15	dogs
16	claws, parents, weeks
17	brush, coat, tool
18	doctor, medicine
21	attention

Published by Lightbox Learning Inc.
276 5th Avenue, Suite 704 #917
New York, NY 10001
Website: www.openlightbox.com

Library of Congress Control Numbe: 2023944851

ISBN 978-1-7911-5771-5 (hardcover)
ISBN 978-1-7911-5772-2 (softcover)
ISBN 978-1-7911-5773-9 (multi-user eBook)

082023
100922

Printed in Guangzhou, China
1 2 3 4 5 6 7 8 9 0 27 26 25 24 23

Project Coordinator: Sara Cucini
Art Director: Terry Paulhus
Layout: Mandy Christiansen and Sushant Deshpande

Every reasonable effort has been made to trace ownership and to obtain permission to reprint copyright material. The publisher would be pleased to have any errors or omissions brought to its attention so that they may be corrected in subsequent printings.

The publisher acknowledges Alamy, Getty Images, and Shutterstock as its primary image suppliers for this title.